CH00544145

A

HUG

IN A

BOOK

To my mum Alessandra and my dad Luca, it's your love and encouragement that got me here.

And to my best friend Cameron, none of this would be possible without you.

A

HUG

IN A

BOOK

Everyday self-care & comforting rituals

My
Self-Love
Supply

contents

PART 3

Body

PART 4

Soul

Building self-care habits

PART 1

intro

Welcome to your friendly and helpful guide to self-care! Let this book be the place you come to for a moment of calm. Use it to help you discover new ways to care for yourself and how you can start using them to build a lifestyle that prioritises your happiness and wellbeing.

A Hug in a Book has been created to provide you with many self-care ideas and engaging activities that make self-care easy and simple. Split into three chapters – mind, body and soul – this book will teach and guide you through many different self-care practices and activities. All of this practical advice has been categorised by a specific self-care area and the estimated time it will take to complete the activity, so no matter what you like to do or how much time you have, there will always be something you can try.

Written by the founder of My Self-Love Supply™, Sofia Pellaschiar, this book embodies a message of self-love and positivity, with inspiration taken from the well-known Instagram page, **@myselflovesupply.**

What is self-care?

Any action that improves your mental, emotional or physical health can be considered self-care. You can think of it as all the actions and decisions that go towards benefitting your health, happiness and wellbeing.

In this book, self-care practices are separated into three focused areas:

Mind – Everything relating to your mental self-care within the areas of organisation, goal-setting, journaling and mindfulness.

Body – Caring for yourself physically, through different self-care activities in the areas of movement, general health, rest and pastimes.

Soul – Looking after your emotional wellbeing by listening to and caring for your emotions and feelings through activities in the areas of self-talk, setting boundaries and connecting with your support network.

You might have heard about self-care as a term associated with 'treating yourself' in a materialistic and expensive sense. The reality of self-care is very different, though. Self-care isn't about luxury and indulgence, it's about attending to your needs with the goal of improving your happiness, wellness and mental health. It's about caring for your mind, body and soul by implementing small and simple habits into your lifestyle that support your wellbeing.

It is important to know that self-care can be very subjective and personal, and therefore it can look different for everyone. No one knows you better than yourself, so only you can truly explore what brings you joy and what improves your wellbeing. An activity that brings someone else peace and calm might be something that you find boring and unhelpful, so remember that when it comes to your self-care journey, *you* are the expert. While there are so many self-care ideas and trends, don't feel that you need to just follow popular advice, instead try to experiment with ideas with the intention of finding what works best for you!

How is self-care good for you?

It's easy to put yourself last when life gets busy and things become stressful. It's perfectly okay that you sometimes struggle to prioritise your needs. Regardless of where you are in life, caring for yourself shouldn't be a luxury, an afterthought – or even a guilt trip.

Self-care is about actionable, practical and realistic lifestyle choices that can improve the quality of your days. It's important to try to care for each and every aspect of wellbeing so that you can build a lifestyle that fosters health and happiness. So much of mainstream 'healthy living' is focused around fitness and dietary health, which is important, but equally as important is your mental health and emotional wellbeing. Self-care can be used both as a preventative and interventional practice to support your general wellbeing. This book will encourage you to explore different self-care practices and guide you through simple ways in which you can build these into your daily routine.

HERE ARE SOME BENEFITS TO EMBARKING ON YOUR SELF-CARE JOURNEY:

- It allows you to be more self-aware and connected with yourself and your needs.

- It can help protect your mental health when times are tough.

- It gives you a wholesome way to prioritise your health and happiness.

- It can help you build better relationships with others, as you'll have more to give.

SELF-CARE JOURNEY: DOS & DON'TS

Do	Don't
Stay flexible and be prepared to change and adapt your plan along the way.	Don't make your self-care schedule too busy and overwork yourself – keep it simple!
Schedule in free time, sometimes doing nothing at all is the most productive thing you can do.	Don't force yourself to enjoy your self-care time. If you don't enjoy it, change it until you do. Self-care should not be a chore.
Keep changing your routine every now and again and try some new self-care practices.	Don't be hard on yourself if you slip up. Just try to get back on track as soon as you are ready.

Caring for yourself shouldn't be a luxury or an afterthought

PART 2
mind

This chapter focuses on the wellbeing of your mind, often referred to as mental self-care. The goal of mental self-care is to provide your mind with activities that foster stimulation, relaxation and resilience. By intentionally performing these self-care practices, you can target each area with the purpose of supporting your mental wellbeing and stimulating your personal growth. Mental self-care encourages you to develop your mind, helping you to realise and develop mental skills that can aid you in everyday life.

The types of mental self-care that we will explore as part of this chapter are:

- Organisation

- Journaling

- Mindfulness

- Goal-setting

Organisation

Your mind benefits from order and simplicity. This is because limiting distractions gives you fewer decisions to think about, allowing you more mental clarity and focus. With this clearer mindset follows many more positives: your productivity will improve, you may experience less stress and you will get that empowering sense of being in control. Organisation is something that can easily become neglected or forgotten about during a hectic day, but this is understandable; it can be difficult to keep on track when your time and energy sometimes need to take priority. The key to an organised lifestyle is to cultivate healthy habits that can help you manage and take control of your day-to-day activities and responsibilities. This will allow you to integrate organisation into your life, without it costing you too much mental energy. There are a lot of different ways in which you can do this, but whatever approach you choose, it should always be done with the intent of improving order or creating simplicity in your life.

Organise your workspace

Organising your workspace can bring you incredible benefits in terms of improved productivity and workflow, and a quick tidy can be achieved in as little as five minutes. A tidy and supportive space will promote clarity of mind, helping you to feel more relaxed and focused on what you wish to accomplish. Physical clutter that has gathered on your workspace is going to send you into a frenzy of distractions. The more objects there are around you, the more likely you are to mentally distance yourself from your original task. Opposite are some other ways in which you can create a more optimal workspace; always be on the lookout for new ways and things that you think might help your productivity and focus.

WORKSPACE TIPS

Keep it clear — take all non-essential things off your desk; nothing promotes clarity better than a blank slate.

Add a board — keep track of your upcoming deadlines, to-do list and projects by fixing a writing board in clear view.

Keep some decor — don't be afraid to personalise your space with a little decor, just make sure that these items foster feelings of warmth and positivity.

Adjust the lighting — appropriate lighting can help your eyes feel more rested. Make the most of natural light and consider adding an extra lamp to your space.

Make decluttering a habit — save five minutes at the end of the day to clear out all the things that are no longer needed, ask yourself, 'what do I need to find here tomorrow morning?'

Tidy up your digital space

We've talked about your physical workspace, but a disorganised digital space can also make for a disorganised mind. Your digital space includes all the apps, social media and storage on your digital devices. To have a good experience when spending time in your digital world, it's necessary to be mindful of how you organise it. Decluttering your digital space simply means making sure that everything you want to use is easy to access, and what you no longer use is archived, deleted, unsubscribed to or unfollowed. Set yourself a timer for 15 minutes – if your digital space is overloaded it's easy to get lost in action!

HOW TO CLEAN UP YOUR DIGITAL SPACE

Declutter apps – delete all apps that you no longer use, so that the ones you do need are easy to find and ready to use.

Simplify your inbox – unsubscribe to all unwanted email newsletters and favourite the emails that you wish to come back to.

Tidy your digital desktop – create folders that make it easy for you to find your work, documents and projects.

Choose your notifications – these can be highly disruptive, so choose to only hear about the things that matter most to you – the rest can wait.

Refresh your social media – unfollow accounts that don't bring you inspiration, growth, laughter or education. Pay particular attention to accounts that engender bad feelings, or that make you feel badly about yourself – they don't serve your wellbeing and they have no place in your new self-care digital world.

Give your belongings a purpose

When tidying, decluttering or reorganising your home, try to be mindful that each of your belongings should bring your life some form of value. There are many ways in which an item can provide value: you might have a use for it, it might look decorative, or it could be sentimental and hold positive memories. Anything that fails to bring value might be better off taken out of your space altogether. Spending just half an hour ridding your home of clutter and 'space-filler' items will allow your living space to become a more relaxed and simple environment. This also gives you the added benefits of needing to clean up less often, being able to find things more easily, and provide more space to bring things that you love into your home.

SHOULD YOU THROW AWAY AN ITEM?

'Have I used it in the last 3 months?'

yes

no

'Do I need to keep this for a specific reason?'

yes

no

'Does it bring me positive feelings, emotions or memories?'

yes

no

'Would my life be negatively affected if I no longer owned this?'

yes

no

Keep it!

Dump it, donate it, sell it or repurpose it!

23

Journaling

Think of journaling as a self-care practice that allows you to express yourself without fear of judgement. Your journal should be your safe space, where you are comfortable sharing all of your thoughts, feelings and emotions as ink on a page, taking them out of the refuge of your mind and setting them free. It can sometimes be confusing to determine what journaling actually involves and how it can be practised to your advantage. The truth is that journaling takes a wide variety of forms and can be used to benefit almost all areas of your self-care. Perhaps you do it to look after your emotional wellbeing by reflecting on feelings and emotions? Or you might journal as a way to focus on your mental wellbeing by writing down your thoughts and thinking about your day.

Brain dump

A brain dump is a journaling technique that involves scribbling down all your thoughts and feelings onto a blank page. It sounds almost too simple, but doing this will help you to create a sense of release, expelling all the clutter and chaos in your mind and letting it breathe. This is a great five-minute practice for the start or end of the day, or just whenever you begin to feel overwhelmed. Never be critical of what you write during a brain dump, this is just an exercise designed to let your thoughts flow.

HOW TO BRAIN DUMP

Grab your journal and a pen.

Set a timer for how long to write for. Aim for two minutes to start with, then increase this as you get more comfortable.

Begin with a simple starter sentence, a general thought from the day perhaps.

Write whatever pops into your mind; it doesn't need to tell a story and it doesn't need to make sense. Let the random thoughts in your mind control what you write on the page.

Try not to let your pen leave the paper. This will prompt your thoughts to flow better, which is exactly what you want.

Take a few moments at the end of your brain dump to read and reflect upon what came up for you.

End–of–day recap

The end-of-day recap journaling technique is very similar to keeping a personal diary. It's the perfect way to introduce yourself to journaling and is a simple addition to any evening routine, which only takes fifteen minutes of your time. What makes this technique different from a diary is that not only do you describe key events in your day, you can also reflect upon the feelings and emotions you experienced during these times. Taking a moment to think about how different situations affected you can be a helpful tool in better understanding yourself and realising why you felt the way that you did. This self-awareness practice can be used to build up your mental resilience so that you are prepared if similar situations and feelings arise again and so you will know how to respond in a way that supports your self-care.

HOW TO DO AN END-OF-DAY RECAP

Sit down in the evening, cast your mind back over the day and write about what comes to you. How much you write, what you write and how you write is totally up to you. To get started, just write down how you felt in the morning!

THINGS YOU COULD
MENTION IN YOUR RECAP

- People you met.

- Conversations you had.

- Something that negatively affected you.

- Something that made you smile.

- Things you would have done differently.

- Things you did well.

- Observations that caught your attention.

- World news.

Scrapbooking

Scrapbooking is one of the best ways to preserve positive memories and bring your journal to life. It's similar to a written journal but with the main content being photos and souvenirs. These photos can be accompanied by as much or as little writing as you like, to give further context and thought to each, and can be updated in half-hour sessions whenever you have something to add. The type of content you choose to use will have a big impact on the vibe of your journal. You might only use photos that show the highlights of your life or those that spark positive emotions. Having a positivity focused scrapbook is perfect to look back on if you want to relive happy memories and lift your mood.

TOP TIPS

- Think of your scrapbook as a storytelling tool, and let this be your creative outlet.

- Don't limit yourself to photos, add sentimental items like movie, concert or travel tickets.

- Pick items that spark an emotion. In your written comment, mention the way the memory makes you feel.

- Get creative with the design and make the most important things stand out with different shapes and colours.

Mindfulness

To be mindful is to be fully present in the moment. It's about being aware of what's around you – the noises, the movements, the fresh air – with all your senses working in harmony to take in your environment. This seems simple, but how often are you in a completely mindful state? Walking along with headphones on or obsessing over some trivial thought in your head is not being mindful. True mindfulness is taking time to listen and let your surroundings speak to you. Mindfulness is a self-care skill, and it will take some practice to get good at, but once you get familiar with the idea, the benefits will come to you. Focusing your mental and emotional energy on what's around you allows you to take a quick break from the rest of your life and focus on the immediate present. This can help to reduce any stress or anxiety that you may be experiencing.

Mindfulness meditation

Mindfulness meditation is an exercise that's intended to slow your mind and control your attention, allowing for relaxation into a state of calm. There's actually no time limit on how long your mindfulness meditation practice can be, but most people find five minutes is an achievable length that's still hugely beneficial. This is a fantastic tool for giving yourself a mental break, and it encourages you to draw your focus away from busy thoughts to the present moment.

There are a few different ways in which you can perform this kind of practice, but as a variation of standard meditation the most common approaches involve stillness and deep breathing.

HOW TO GET STARTED WITH MINDFULNESS MEDITATION

Find some time away from your responsibilities, when you won't be interrupted.

Position yourself comfortably and make sure that your posture is good.

Begin by relaxing your muscles and taking slow, deep breaths. Concentrate on every breath in and every breath out.

The goal of this exercise is simply to control your thoughts and bring your attention to the present moment. If a thought pops into your mind, observe it and let it pass by as you return your mind to the present.

When you feel ready, slowly lift your gaze. Peacefully stretch out all of your body as you take in the surrounding sounds, colours and smells. Pay attention to how you feel after the exercise.

Create a mindful environment

A useful self-care skill that you can learn and try out is creating a mindful environment. This involves changing the space you are in to reflect an aura of peace and calm. You can change your environment in many ways depending on what relaxes your mind the most, and it doesn't need to take up much time. You can do this visually, by filling your walls with imagery that brings you feelings of positivity. Adjusting the lighting is another way to change the mood of a room; you can let in natural light for an awake and energised vibe, or have a darker room with only one lamp on for a more relaxed mood. Comforting atmospheres can also be created with scented candles or plants – these will freshen the air around you, helping your space reflect the mood you want to foster.

QUICK AND EASY WAYS TO
CHANGE THE MOOD OF A ROOM

Appearance

Decorate your walls with imagery that lifts
your mood.

Focus on having colours that promote relaxation.

Try to keep your surfaces clean and uncluttered.

Atmosphere

Light a scented candle.

Add some plants or flowers

Open a window and let in some fresh air.

Comfort

Make sure that where you sit or lie is comfortable.

Use soft and warm materials wherever you can.

Position your furniture to give you the most
space possible.

Embracing nature

Spending time in nature can be incredibly beneficial for your mind, body and soul, as it can lower your stress levels and help you to feel more connected to the present moment. Try to plan a half hour when you can immerse yourself in a natural space close to where you live, full of trees, wildlife, flowers or amazing views. Doing this does not have to be complicated, being in nature can just mean going for a wander in a nearby woodland, park or a beach. Try to use your senses to connect with the nature around you by putting your bare feet into the grass and taking mindful breaths of fresh air. Sunlight can also bring its own set of benefits, such as increasing the production of vitamin D. By all means don't limit yourself to just thirty minutes, but if half an hour is all you can spare it is still more than enough to feel the benefits.

TEN DIFFERENT WAYS IN WHICH YOU CAN ENJOY NATURE

Walk around your local park.

Sunbathe at the nearest beach.

Have a picnic.

Walk a trail you've never been on before.

Buy plants for your home.

Nurture your own garden.

Find as many wild flowers as you can.

Walk along a beach or a river.

Do some wildlife/nature photography.

Visit your closest natural wonder.

Goal-setting

A goal can be described as an outcome that you wish to achieve; this can be something big, such as learning a new language; or something simpler, such as having a productive morning. No matter how long it takes you, or how complex it might be, all goals are worthy of celebration. Accomplishing your goals isn't always easy but having a success plan will give you the best chance. One way to do this is goal-setting, a strategy that involves dividing your larger goal into smaller, more manageable targets and checkpoints to make it easier for you to follow the path towards achieving your ambition. Goal-setting is amazing for self-development, as it allows you to have a clear vision of what you want to achieve, then gives you the motivation and direction you need to get there. Without targets or plans in place, it can be easy to lose sight of your long-term vision.

To-do list

To-do lists are a simple yet impactful addition to your morning routine. Simply described, they are a list of everything and anything that you wish to accomplish throughout the day. Each time you complete a task, it gets ticked off or crossed out. These little lists are such a powerful tool because they help you to visualise your progress. Spending five minutes writing a list will not only give you clarity on how you plan to organise your day, but it also helps you to better manage your time during and between tasks.

The biggest benefit of to-do lists is their ability to motivate. The sense of satisfaction and accomplishment that comes from ticking off a task will help to encourage you to start further tasks, giving your productivity a welcomed boost!

TO-DO LIST TIPS

Between three and six tasks a day is manageable and realistic – the list doesn't have to be too long, and the tasks don't have to be big.

Put the task that is most critical right at the top of the list. Try to tackle that one as early in the day as possible to get it out the way!

Try to write or review your to-do list in the morning, before you start your day.

Make a big deal out of accomplishing a task; tick it off in a big green pen or scribble it all out. Use this motivation to work through your list.

Letter to your future self

Writing a letter to your future self is an exercise that will allow you to spend some time reflecting on your vision of the future and where you wish to see yourself in one, five or even twenty years' time. This process can help you develop ideas around the goals you want to accomplish and allow you to begin to visualise the journey towards the future you aspire to. Writing a letter also means that you can store it for future reference. You can keep it close to you as a regular reminder, or put it away somewhere safe and open it on a future date that you have set. It can be fun to reflect upon what you have achieved, what has shifted and how your dreams have developed over time. But remember, just because something didn't work out as you had imagined, it doesn't mean it was a bad outcome.

HOW TO WRITE A LETTER
TO YOUR FUTURE SELF

Brainstorm — Let your imagination run wild and scribble down some goals, visions, hopes and dreams. Just list whatever pops into your mind.

Visualise — Picture yourself years into the future (the timescale is up to you). What do you see?

Write — Tell your future self about your goals and how you plan to achieve them. Mention your worries, ambitions, motivation and current life situation.

30-MINUTE SELF-CARE
Vision board

A vision board is a collection of images that represent a goal you hope to achieve or the life you are striving for. Vision boards are a powerful tool to help you better connect with your goals, offering you regular inspiration and motivation. Allow yourself half an hour for this exercise, to really focus on what you feel is most important for you to achieve and how best to illustrate it. Be mindful to choose only the images that remind you of your goal, fill your soul with inspiration, that you never tire of looking at or which motivate you every day to push through those hard moments. The aim is to help you find clarity and maintain focus on what you want to achieve. It's important that you put your vision board somewhere in clear sight so that it is often in view – on your bedroom wall or smartphone lock screen, for example. This way, you can always keep your dreams to the front of your mind, motivating you to make those small choices every day that will get you one step closer to your end goal.

INSPIRATION FOR YOUR VISION BOARD

Places you want to travel to.

Relationships you want to have.

Home and family life.

Career and finance goals.

Business ambitions.

Personal growth (such as hobbies or education).

Health targets.

Any of your other personal ambitions.

Mind self-care checklist

SELF-CARE	ACTIVITY	HAVE I TRIED IT?	HOW DID I FIND IT? (X/10)
ORGANISATION	Organise your workspace		
	Tidy up your digital space		
	Give your belongings a purpose		
JOURNALING	Brain dump		
	End-of-day recap		
	Scrapbooking		

SELF-CARE	ACTIVITY	HAVE I TRIED IT?	HOW DID I FIND IT? (X/10)
MINDFULNESS	Mindfulness meditation		
	Create a mindful environment		
	Embracing nature		
GOAL-SETTING	To-do list		
	Letter to your future self		
	Vision board		

PART 3
body

This chapter is all about looking after your body, also known as physical self-care. Physical self-care has a wide impact on many aspects of your overall wellbeing, from your mood and energy levels to your mind–body connection. Good physical wellbeing doesn't mean running marathons and eating perfectly every single day, it is about making those balanced lifestyle choices that will have a positive impact on your body's health and wellness. Amazing progress can be made through small and consistent changes to your daily routine, resulting in a balanced and enjoyable approach to physical self-care.

The types of physical self-care that we will explore as part of this chapter are:

♥   Movement

♥   Body care

♥   Rest

♥   Pastimes

Movement

Movement is simply about moving your body; not necessarily in a particular way or at a particular intensity, the only thing that matters is that your body gets adequate movement every day. The activities that you choose to do will be very dependent upon your lifestyle, ability and what you enjoy – and that's perfectly okay. There is something for everyone. It's important to make this part of your lifestyle enjoyable, too – do only the activities that you like and occasionally vary them with different scenery, upbeat music and good company. The options and wellbeing benefits are endless.

Quick stretch session

The benefits on the body that even a quick five-minute stretch can give you are amazing (yoga, Pilates and similar included). Particularly after long periods of being still, such as during work or first thing in the morning, a gentle stretch can loosen you up and energise your body. Not only will stretching improve your flexibility and maintain your mobility, but it will also release a lot of unwanted tension throughout your body.

THREE EASY WAYS TO STRETCH

♥ Stand with your feet together, hands in the air.
Holding your arms straight, slowly reach down and
try to touch your toes. You may not be able to reach,
so only go as far as is comfortable. Hold this position
for 20 seconds, then slowly come back up.

♥ Place yourself in the middle of an open doorway.
Stretch your arms across each side of the
doorframe. Gently lean forward, using your forearms
to support your weight. You should feel a deep
stretch across your chest and shoulders.

♥ With your feet shoulder-width apart, lower yourself
into a squat position. Hold this squat for as long as
it feels comfortable. If you need to hold on to
something for assistance, this is recommended.

Movement mindset

One of the most common reasons why it can be hard to achieve your daily movement goals is a lack of time in your daily routine. This is a perfectly valid problem that so many people struggle with, but remember being active is not always about finding an hour to spend in the gym, sometimes just fifteen minutes and a daily task is all you need. The simple solution is to change your mindset towards movement and how you perform your habitual chores. The goal here is to prioritise movement whenever possible and always be looking for opportunities to move your body.

This doesn't have to be anything more than getting out of your desk chair and walking over to your bottle of water to help give your body the action it craves. Once you're up, you might as well keep walking and

MOVEMENT MINDSET SWITCHES

Driving	$\rightarrow$	Cycling
Getting the bus	$\rightarrow$	Walking
Sitting desk	$\rightarrow$	Standing desk
Lift	$\rightarrow$	Stairs
Normal watch	$\rightarrow$	Fitness watch
Shop online	$\rightarrow$	Shop in store
Park close to your destination	$\rightarrow$	Park further away

maybe perform a couple of household tasks before you sit back down. Fitness watches are also a great addition to your life, allowing you to track your steps so that you can set a daily movement goal and consistently meet it.

Getting sweaty

Different workouts suit different people. If you want exercise to become a consistent part of your lifestyle, you need to focus on making it enjoyable for you. With that being said, the occasional workout should be something that you try to include in your life because of the amazing positives it will have on both your physical and mental health. For some people, hard-and-fast gym sessions make them feel energised, but for others, quite the opposite. So only do what is right for you. As a very loose rule of thumb, if your workout is making you a little hot and sweaty, then you're probably working at a good intensity to achieve lots of wellbeing benefits.

WORKOUTS THAT YOU MIGHT FIND FUN

♥ Hiking

♥ Outdoor cycling

♥ Swimming

♥ Social sports

♥ Your outdoor hobbies

♥ Animal spotting

♥ Home workout

♥ Fitness class

♥ Dancing

Body care

Body care refers to all of the things that you consume (food and drinks), your physical health and your hygiene. Body care is probably the area of your wellbeing that you currently pay most attention to in a typical day, as it is an essential part of being human. Just because you already care for this aspect of your wellbeing does not mean that there isn't room for improvements. The most caring approach to healthy living focuses on balance and consistency. With this you can achieve really positive outcomes whilst still allowing yourself the freedom of choice. If big lifestyle changes are needed (which they sometimes are), it's often best to slowly add these into your life gradually, to help you adapt and remain consistent. Remember to never be too hard on yourself when you slip up – progress is an up-and-down journey. Trust that your small steps forward and your determination will improve your wellbeing for some time to come.

Water intake

Essential to every single function in your entire body is water. You need it to feel and perform at your best each and every day. With this in mind, do you pay close enough attention to the amount of water you drink? The key to consuming a healthy quantity is to simply drink regularly throughout the day so that you never feel thirsty. Set yourself a daily target, and if it feels too much or too little, then you can adjust it the next day. Make this as easy on yourself as possible so you can follow the same habit daily.

SIMPLE TIPS TO MAKE THIS EASIER

Have one big bottle that you fill in the morning and sip from throughout the day.

Drink a big glass of water first thing in the morning to start your day off well.

Flavour your water with lemon or juice so that it is more tempting for you to drink.

Consider herbal teas and camomile as a water supplement during the cold winter period.

Avoid drinking lots of water too late in the evening as this may disrupt your sleep.

Health check–in

Self-care is also being aware of your body's health and being proactive when it comes to caring for it. It's not uncommon to experience issues that may have been unexpected, and some of the time these will require medical assistance for you to get better. The most caring thing that you can do for yourself is to check in with your body so you become aware of possible problems and seek specialist help as soon as you possibly can. Your health is not a burden to medical professionals, so never feel guilty for asking for advice and making your health a priority.

WAYS YOU CAN CHECK
IN WITH YOUR HEALTH

♥ Book a general check-in appointment with
your doctor.

♥ Seek support early if you are struggling with your
mental health.

♥ Be aware of breast changes.

♥ Track any health changes or symptoms that you
may experience by writing them down in a diary.

♥ Get your questions answered by a professional
– they are there to help.

Meal prepping

Finding free time to do all those things that boost your wellbeing can be a challenge – especially with a busy work–life schedule. By taking advantage of small lifestyle changes, such as prepping meals in advance, you can start to use your time and energy in the ways that you want. Meal preparation simply means making a meal ahead of time so it's ready when you want it. Some people like to do a big batch-cook on the weekend when they have a few spare hours, but not everyone enjoys spending that long in the kitchen. In just thirty minutes you can cook a recipe for later, even multiplying the quantities so that you can portion up a few meals and store them in the fridge for use throughout the week – saving you all the time and hassle of cooking on busy nights. You could also just pop these meals in the freezer for when you don't have the time or energy to make anything! Other quick and easy ways to get ahead with meal prep are either to prepare your lunch the night before or make an extra portion of dinner to take to work the next day.

HOW TO MEAL PREP

💜 Plan which meals you want to make and buy the ingredients.

💜 Schedule some cooking time into your weekend.

💜 Batch-cook large amounts of the same meal.

💜 Separate your food equally among tubs and put them in the freezer.

💜 Enjoy your home-cooked 'ready meal' whenever you need it!

Rest

Rest is about sleep, relaxation and recovery – three types of self-care that all support your wellbeing in their own way. The value of getting adequate rest is so often taken for granted, with priority going to squeezing every last waking second out of the day. But your body is not a machine and it shouldn't be treated like one. After long or intense periods of work, it's common for the mind and body to become fatigued and burned out. When this happens, productivity, motivation and energy all start to tumble. Always be mindful that overworking isn't healthy and can commonly be a cause of stress and low mood, so take a break – even five minutes is enough to hit the refresh button. A moment out of the busyness of the day will allow you to recharge, helping to protect your mental health and wellbeing over the long term. Sometimes doing nothing for a little while can be the most productive thing you can do, so never feel guilty for having a much-needed rest.

Calming the senses

One common type of fatigue you can experience is sensory overload. This is when your senses become overwhelmed with too much information, such as different sounds and sights. Typical places where you could experience this are city centres, new environments, amusement parks and airports, but it's even possible to have sensory fatigue from simply sitting with your phone for too long. It's good to take a few minutes every so often to relax your senses and give your mind a break. This could be done by moving into a quieter environment or switching off your electronic devices for a while to reduce distraction. A good practice that can help ease all your senses at once is to perform a simple breathing exercise.

BREATHING EXERCISE GUIDE

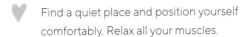 Find a quiet place and position yourself comfortably. Relax all your muscles.

Close your eyes and take a deep breath in through your nose. Allow your belly to fill with air.

Gently exhale through your nose.

Now place one hand on your belly. As you breathe in, feel your belly rise up.

Hold your breath for a moment, then slowly release it, and as you do so, feel your belly lower.

Repeat this process until your mind has rested and you feel calmer.

Recovery time

Some days are exhausting, and being mentally and physically switched on from dusk to dawn can sometimes just be too much. To help combat this, think about planning a period of recharge into your day. This is commonly done in the form of a nap, but naps aren't for everyone and there are more ways than one to rest your mind and body. Partaking in something relaxing or anything less taxing on your body – even getting out for a short stroll and some fresh air – might be just what you need to make it through to the end of the day. It can be challenging to find a period of free time during a workday or busy family lifestyle, but allocating just fifteen minutes to slowing down your day is vital for you to keep performing at your very best!

WAYS TO SLOW DOWN AND RECHARGE

Slow down

 Avoid multitasking.

 Take a break from technology.

 Do something less challenging.

Recharge

 Take a power nap.

 Have a coffee break.

 Go for a relaxing walk while listening to music.

Evening unwind

The final few hours of the evening should be about unwinding and preparing yourself for a good night's sleep, and too much mental stimulation or stressful thoughts during this time could have a really negative effect on the quality of your sleep. If you know you have a busy day ahead, be mindful of this and try to structure your time accordingly to allow yourself just half an hour later to unwind your mind and body for the night ahead. This is best done by scheduling harder tasks in the beginning of the day and easier tasks towards the evening. Even a little bit of relaxation helps to clear your mind of unhelpful thoughts and concerns about the following day – this kind of thinking will only rob you of your much-needed rest.

Things to *try* in the evening	**Things to *avoid* in the evening**
Lavender aromatherapy	Thought-provoking exercises or work
Read a novel	High-energy food (such as sugary foods and coffee)
Sit in gentle, dim lighting	Too much screen time

Pastimes

Everyone can have some form of pastime; an activity that you do purely for fun, enjoyment or satisfaction. In your daily routine, shrouded with responsibilities, it's good to make the most of any free time you can find. A pastime to occupy this part of your day is a perfect solution that will also have a huge positive impact on your wellbeing, allowing you to put a beneficial purpose to your spare minutes. The best way to spark new interests, hobbies and passions is to explore different things. The world is rich with opportunities and possibilities, yet it can be so easy to miss what is right in front of you. Your next pastime could be right around the corner or a website click away. The activities in this section are intended to encourage you to try new activities and spend your free time doing something you enjoy.

Plan some fun time

Use your free time on days off or in the evenings to spend five minutes connecting with loved ones, or perhaps coming up with a plan to visit somewhere new or do something fun. There are endless wellbeing benefits to doing this, such as relationship building, physical activity, adventure and rejuvenation – to name but a few. Part of the enjoyment in this process is in the planning; as with organising a holiday, there's excitement to be had in exploring your options and opening your mind to new possibilities. Try to set yourself a goal of two or three fun weekend activities each month. Make sure to vary it up each time with new people, places and experiences!

FUN WEEKEND IDEAS YOU CAN PLAN IN 5 MINUTES

- Taking a nature hike.

- Having a picnic.

- Making a road trip.

- Finding a maze to explore.

- Choosing a historical site to visit.

- Finding somewhere to camp or lodge.

- Planning a day out at the beach.

- Checking your community calendar for fun local events.

15-MINUTE SELF-CARE
Rediscover an old passion

Change is normal throughout your different life stages.
Your lifestyle changes, your mindset changes and your
interests change. Passions that you once had in years
gone by often get lost and locked away as memories.
Having an activity that sparks your excitement is
important for your wellbeing; it offers you a sanctuary
where you can escape from daily life and just immerse
yourself within a period of bliss. So setting aside fifteen
minutes to reconnect with something that you used
to love doing can be a great way to say hello to a past
version of yourself and maybe even rediscover a
former enthusiasm.

The world
is rich with
possibilities &
opportunities

ADVICE FOR REDISCOVERING
AN OLD PASSION

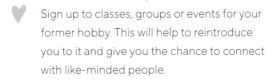

♥ Sign up to classes, groups or events for your former hobby. This will help to reintroduce you to it and give you the chance to connect with like-minded people.

♥ Don't force yourself to like something. It's okay if you no longer take enjoyment from things that you once used to.

♥ Try getting involved in a different way. It's expected that you may not have the ability or desire that you once had, but that doesn't have to stop you. There are always alternative opportunities to get involved, such as coaching, teaching or spectating.

Learn a new skill

Learning a new skill, no matter how complex or useful, is a fantastic way for you to promote self-development. It can be a quirky party trick, a new technique or a lifelong desire that you've never got around to fulfilling. The point is, it doesn't matter what you try because the processes will remain the same. Learning a new skill can be a daunting prospect when you're a total beginner but you might surprise yourself how quickly you will improve with just thirty minutes' practice a few times a week. The journey will also allow you to develop some of your personal qualities – such as patience, resilience and confidence. You may also find that the journey doesn't just stop with your new skill. Perhaps it leads you into learning further skills or even opens up new doors of opportunity for you. Never underestimate the value of self-development, because you never know how much you might grow or the journey it might take you on.

NEW SKILL IDEAS

♥ Learn how to draw.

♥ Learn some common phrases from a new language.

♥ Take a photography class.

♥ Master some basic self-defence.

♥ Learn some breathing techniques.

♥ Find out how to start your own business.

♥ Learn an instrument.

♥ Get to grips with some very basic car repair.

Body self-care checklist

SELF-CARE	ACTIVITY	HAVE I TRIED IT?	HOW DID I FIND IT? (X/10)
MOVEMENT	Quick stretch session		
	Movement mindset		
	Getting sweaty		
BODY CARE	Water intake		
	Health check-in		
	Meal prepping		

SELF-CARE	ACTIVITY	HAVE I TRIED IT?	HOW DID I FIND IT? (X/10)
REST	Calming the senses		
	Recovery time		
	Evening unwind		
PASTIMES	Plan some fun time		
	Rediscover an old passion		
	Learn a new skill		

PART 4

soul

This chapter focuses on the soul – the area connected with listening to and caring for your emotions and feelings. Self-care associated with the soul, known as emotional wellbeing, can be practised with intentions of shifting your mindset and understanding your emotions. It's about paying attention to and honouring the emotional state you are in. Through mindset reframing and emotional connection with yourself and others, you can gently shift the way you think and feel about the world around you into more helpful perspectives.

The types of emotional self-care that we will explore as part of this chapter are:

 Boundaries

 Gratitude

 Self-talk

 Connection

Boundaries

Having boundaries is a form of self-care that helps you to protect your emotional wellbeing. Everybody has their own personal needs and limits, and you should not feel guilty (or be made to feel guilty) for making these a priority within your relationships. Boundaries are something you establish between yourself and someone else (or others) to give you physical space or emotional protection. In a physical sense, this could be as simple as closing a door so that you have some space to reflect by yourself. When spoken about emotionally, boundaries are put in place to help you protect your feelings, beliefs and needs from external demands you may find uncomfortable. They can be thought of as guidelines and expectations for relationships that all parties understand and this sets out the communication for what is acceptable and tolerable for you.

Saying 'no'

A big part of protecting and caring for your emotional wellbeing is allowing yourself to say 'no' to others, without those feelings of guilt. Declining an invitation or turning your phone on silent is not selfish, it's simply creating a boundary between your needs and other people's wants. Your reasoning might be that your body needs rest; you're not in the right mindset to socialise; or that you simply just don't want to go. Whatever it might be, you deserve to prioritise these feelings and needs. It's okay to want time to yourself and it's okay to communicate to others that you don't want to do something.

REASONS YOU COULD HAVE FOR SAYING 'NO'

You just don't want to.

You need some time to yourself.

You don't want to socialise.

You'd rather prioritise yourself.

The person asking is impacting negatively on your wellbeing.

Your intuition is telling you so.

You're tired.

You'd rather do something else.

Boundaries with others

Establishing boundaries with others is important, as they help you to remain within your comfortable limits in any given situation. At first it may feel selfish or rude to set boundaries with people, but in the long term this usually promotes healthy and respectful relationships with the people you communicate with, by allowing you both to feel comfortable and safe at all times. It's normal to set different types of boundaries, depending on the type of relationship you have with that person – such as a family member, medical professional, colleague, loved one, friend, neighbour/roommate, etc. Creating your personal boundary can be done in a really brief conversation and involves identifying acts or conversations with which you are not comfortable within that relationship, then outlining rules that make it clear where those limits lie.

EXAMPLES OF BOUNDARIES YOU COULD SET WITH DIFFERENT PEOPLE

Colleagues

 No conversations about personal life.

 No physical contact (such as hugs, handshakes).

Family

 Requiring personal space and privacy.

 No debates/arguments on sensitive issues or beliefs.

Friends

 No discussions about certain past events or trigger points.

 Knowledge that you can only be there for them at a certain time.

Hard-choice self-care

Don't just set boundaries with others; you can also set boundaries with yourself. This is about making those hard choices that end up benefitting your wellbeing in the long term. Self-care certainly isn't all pampering yourself, sometimes it's simply about doing what is right for you, even if your temptations are telling you otherwise. This is very much a case of 'actions have consequences', and sometimes those consequences will have a negative effect on your wellbeing, which is why discipline and self-boundaries must be established to protect this. A hard-choice self-care decision could be a rule with yourself to face some recurring stresses as soon as you are able to, rather than delaying them.

DIFFERENT EXAMPLES OF BOUNDARIES
YOU MAY SET WITH YOURSELF

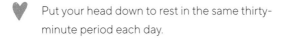

- Put your head down to rest in the same thirty-minute period each day.

- Limit your social media time each day to two half-hour sessions.

- Strictly keep to your budget each month.

- Pay bills when they are due.

- Don't work past 7 pm.

- Keep your work life and personal life separate.

- Limit coffee intake to three cups per day.

Gratitude

Practising gratitude means appreciating all that you have, see or experience in the world around you. It's about pushing aside the noise and finding the positives within every situation. It can be easy to let time float by, paying little attention to the nuances of everyday life. Daily practice of gratitude will give you a chance to refresh your mindset and encourage you to absorb those positive feelings that foster a warm sense of appreciation and positivity about your life. The more you focus your energy on finding positives and joy, the less energy you will have for negatives. Having an appreciative outlook on your daily life can help you find new meanings in the things you once took for granted. A life of gratitude may also help you become more considerate of opportunities to learn and grow and to extend your help to others.

State your gratitudes

This quick and simple daily gratitude exercise can help shift your mindset in an instant. To get started, grab a piece of paper or open the notes app on your phone. Write down three things you are grateful for in that particular moment or from that day. Try to focus on something that is fresh in your mind – a recent event, interaction or situation, for example. This can also extend to objects, your environment or just anything that brings your life value. It might be helpful to look out of a window for inspiration. Describe your gratitudes and take note of the positive emotions that they foster and the value they bring to you. As you get into the habit of being mindful of the good in your life, it will become easier to find even more of it when you are looking!

SIMPLE GRATITUDE IDEAS
TO GET YOU STARTED

♥ Look at the object to your left. How does it bring value to your life?

♥ What is one small thing that you use every day that you could not live without?

♥ List some reasons why you love your home.

♥ What was the last thing to make you smile?

♥ I am grateful for the present moment because...

Write a letter to your past self

It's easy to overlook how much you have accomplished and all the things you so bravely managed to get through. This exercise is about pausing for a moment to appreciate how far you have come in recent months or years. To do this, think back in time to all the things that looked hard, scary or impossible to achieve, no matter how small. Now write a letter to a past version of yourself who was about to face these challenges. It doesn't have to be lengthy, in fifteen minutes you can talk about how you managed to overcome the hard times and how these challenges made you who you are today. Mention all that you learned and how grateful you are that you kept going, no matter how tough it got. This will help you realise your resilience and mental strength, as well as your ability to adapt when things didn't go your way.

HOW TO WRITE TO YOURSELF

💜 Decide on the challenge you want to look back on, or perhaps a past period of your life.

💜 Think back to how you felt at that time about the situation. How did you manage the adversity? How did you pick yourself up when you were down? Describe these thoughts to your past self.

💜 Tell yourself how you feel about that situation now, when it is over. Has it made you grow? Would you change anything? Tell yourself how proud you are of pushing through.

💜 Remember to mention all your accomplishments along the way. They deserve to be celebrated!

Finding a grateful perspective

Daily life can be full of problems and annoyances that can often put a dampener on your day. It doesn't always have to be like this though. Learning to reframe your thinking to reflect a more positive outlook is a powerful practice that can help you navigate life's daily struggles with gratitude and appreciation. Within any situation, challenge or problem, positives can be found if you look with grateful eyes. This exercise encourages you to reframe negatives into positives. You can do this by looking at the situation from a different perspective. Step out of your own shoes and think deeply about each situation with a clean slate. Everything tells a story, but it's up to you which chapter you read.

EXAMPLES OF REFRAMING

A messy house	$----\rightarrow$	A place to call home
Dirty dishes	$----\rightarrow$	Good food to eat
Homework to do	$----\rightarrow$	Future education

PROMPTS FOR YOU TO TRY

Laundry to do	$----\rightarrow$	———————— ————
Paying taxes	$----\rightarrow$	———————— ————————
Getting out of bed	$----\rightarrow$	———————— ————————

Self-talk

Your self-talk is simply your internal dialogue, the voice in your mind that provides you with thoughts, ideas and questions. Self-talk is often a blend of your conscious and subconscious thoughts, and these can sometimes be positive or at other times more negative focused. By becoming more consciously aware of your inner self-critic you can start to reframe your unhelpful thoughts into more balanced and helpful ones. The way you talk to yourself is important and having a positive sense of self contributes to your mental and emotional wellbeing. Humans naturally tend to focus their mental energy more on the negatives, thinking of 'what if?' scenarios and focusing more on what went wrong. It is healthy and normal to have these thoughts and they are beneficial in some circumstances, but if your mind is flooded with this train of thought it can be very difficult to escape it and embrace positivity instead.

Create your own affirmations

Affirmations are positive statements that you can tell yourself with the intention of encouraging a more positive mindset or promoting self-change. They are often used by people to foster the reality they desire, such as making (or attracting) happiness, love, beauty or wealth. To practise affirmations, you should either repetitively write them out or read them aloud. As a beginner's guide, try doing this at least once every day and repeating each affirmation at least five times – easy to do in five minutes while getting ready in the morning or while travelling to work. Everyone has their own preference, though, so experiment with what and when feels comfortable for you.

HOW TO BUILD YOUR
OWN AFFIRMATIONS

Step 1: Identify your desire.

Step 2: Identify what you need to do to achieve your desire.

Step 3: Combine these two statements into a short and impactful affirmation.

EXAMPLES

Step 1	Step 2	Step 3
I want to become a better artist	I need to work hard and practise	My hard work and determination will make me the best artist I can be
I want to feel peaceful and calm	Sticking to my mindfulness meditation practice	My mindfulness meditation routine will make me feel calm

Reframe your negative self-talk

Thoughts are influenced in many ways: your mood, past experiences, beliefs or close connections, to name a few. It can be easy for this self-talk to turn negative and your mental state could be affected, causing you to feel low and anxious. Noticing your negative internal chatter is the first step in reframing your self-talk. Once you have acknowledged these thoughts you can begin to challenge them, think about them rationally and be kind to yourself in the process. Often the first thoughts to pop into your mind are based on subconscious biases or ideas that might not reflect the true situation. While you want to try to reach for a more positive-focused mindset, it's also good to accept that negative thoughts are just a part of being human. However, not all of them are true, but once you become aware of this, you can start reframing more helpful and balanced thoughts.

HOW TO REFRAME YOUR NEGATIVE SELF-TALK

🤍 When you begin to feel overwhelmed by negativity, write a list of all these unhelpful thoughts. Your worries, your self-doubts, your criticisms – let it all out on the page.

🤍 Beside each statement you wrote, write a challenger statement; a statement that holds the same meaning but has a more balanced, kinder tone.

🤍 Example: 'I am lazy, and I will never be successful'. Challenge this thought in your mind and tell yourself, 'My rest is important and is what I need right now, it's my steady progress that will help me reach my goals.'

Practise self-compassion

Practising self-compassion is extending to yourself that kindness, understanding and non-judgement that you extend to others in their time of need. While it is often natural to be extra critical and expectant of yourself, this type of thinking can impact negatively on your mental state. Oftentimes, these expectations and standards are unrealistic and result in damaged confidence and self-belief. If you are not naturally inclined this way, as so many aren't, being compassionate and forgiving of yourself can be challenging. Self-compassion is an exercise that must be practised regularly and intently for you to begin to shift some of those heavy expectations that weigh you down.

One way that self-compassion can be practised is to ask yourself, 'what do I need to hear right now to express kindness to myself?'

AFFIRMATION IDEAS
FOR SELF-COMPASSION

♥ May I give myself the compassion that I need.

♥ May I learn to accept myself as I am.

♥ May I forgive myself.

♥ May I be strong.

♥ May I be patient.

Connection

Connection is about your interaction and relationships with other people, whether they are loved ones, friends, associates or strangers. It is a fundamental part of what it means to be human and it is important for supporting and strengthening both your emotional and mental wellbeing. Connection can come in lots of different forms; you can connect socially, through interaction with people you are familiar with; or even non-verbally, through actions that offer support or kindness. Virtual communication can also be a way to connect with people, but be mindful that technology should be used as a way to support physical connection to others, not replace it. Having a social network of people who care for you should never be taken for granted. Supporting or repairing your wellbeing is tough, and sometimes the most caring thing you can do for yourself is to step back and ask for help.

Perform an act of kindness

One form of connection that you can build is through your actions towards others. Despite an act of kindness usually being an intentionally selfless act, it has actually been proven that this action will also have many benefits for your own wellbeing. Supporting others can foster positive emotions, a sense of purpose and a boost in optimism. Being helpful or kind does not have to be a random or opportunistic event, and it doesn't have to take more than five minutes of your day. It's good to frequently plan small acts of kindness to help support others you love, assist those in need, or just to gift someone a smile to brighten their day. Having a compassionate mindset towards others is good practice for encouraging compassion and kindness within yourself whilst making the world a better place, one little bit of kindness at a time.

ACTS OF KINDNESS IDEAS

♥ Save your spare coins and donate them to a charity at the end of the month.

♥ Make an effort to buy gifts and products from small local businesses.

♥ Write a supportive comment on your friends' Instagram posts.

♥ Compliment someone's outfit.

♥ Offer to help out a neighbour or friend with a big task coming up.

♥ Pass along a compliment to a service worker's boss.

♥ Send an unexpected gift to someone who you think deserves one.

♥ Let your social network know that you're there for them if they need you.

Connect with your support network

Your support network is all the people who care about you and look out for you. Support networks don't have to be big, just a small number of people who would take your hand if you fall down. These kinds of connections are precious, they allow you to feel a sense of protection and belonging that shouldn't be taken for granted if ever your emotional wellbeing is low. It's important that these relationships are maintained, and to do this will require a bit of effort on your part, but not a lot of time. There are many ways to stay connected and you should try to practise them whenever you can. A quick catch-up or a friendly reminder to someone that you care for them is sometimes all that is needed.

WAYS TO CONNECT WITH YOUR
SUPPORT NETWORK

♥ Tell them why you have been thinking about them.

♥ Check in with how they are doing.

♥ Plan an in-person meet-up, if it's possible.

♥ Spontaneously video-call them.

♥ Post an online photo of you both.

♥ Send them a quick text to ask about their day.

30-MINUTE SELF-CARE
Finding new friendships

Over time, social circles change. Some people may come and go from your life very quickly, others might drift away after a lifetime of being close. People change, and so do circumstances, so it's perfectly okay that the group of people you socialise with evolves over time. Part of this comes from making new connections. Not only does this support a healthy social network, but it will also open your mind to new ideas and different outlooks on life that come from having fresh conversations. However, it can be hard to make new friendships, especially if you feel as though you're stuck in your own little bubble, going to the same places and seeing the same people. If this sounds familiar to you, you might want to try some of the suggestions opposite to spark new relationships.

WAYS TO MEET NEW PEOPLE

 Join a club associated with one of your pastimes.

Join a walking group.

Get involved in some volunteering you're passionate about.

Join an online community.

Spark up a conversation at the dog park.

Go to a child-parent event.

Ask a few colleagues out to lunch.

Take part in a class that interests you.

Soul
self–care
checklist

SELF-CARE	ACTIVITY	HAVE I TRIED IT?	HOW DID I FIND IT? (X/10)
BOUNDARIES	Saying 'no'		
	Boundaries with others		
	Hard-choice self-care		
GRATITUDE	State your gratitudes		
	Write a letter to your past self		
	Finding a grateful perspective		

SELF-CARE	ACTIVITY	HAVE I TRIED IT?	HOW DID I FIND IT? (X/10)
SELF-TALK	Create your own affirmations		
	Reframe your negative self-talk		
	Practise self-compassion		
CONNECTION	Perform an act of kindness		
	Connect with your support network		
	Finding new friendships		

Building self-care habits

Self-care habits can be small or more complex, but they will all add up to make positive impacts on your life. To achieve the most benefit possible from your self-care, it is important to practise it regularly and with intention. This often means building some of your most valuable self-care activities into your lifestyle through creating habits. Once a habit is established in your routine, performing it becomes second nature.

That leaves just one question, though... How do you build a self-care habit?

Start by identifying what it is you really want to change and then work on how you can tie these habits to your existing routine. If things feel overwhelming at first, try to break things down into small, more manageable chunks. Once you've successfully incorporated a new habit into your daily life, you can either build on it (like adding another five minutes to your mindfulness practice) or add another new habit.

PUT THIS INTO PRACTICE!

 What self-care activities did you find most helpful?

 What self-care activities did you enjoy the most?

 Pick a few self-care activities that you'd like to build into a habit for each category.

FOR EXAMPLE

 **Mind** – To-do lists, mindfulness meditation

 **Body** – Staying hydrated, movement mindset

 **Soul** – Stating my gratitudes, connecting with my support network

To build these new self-care habits, try to incorporate them into your current routine using this system:

When I *'daily action'*, I will practise my *'new self-care habit'*.

SELF-CARE ROUTINES EXAMPLES

Morning self-care

♥ When I *brush my teeth*, I will *state three things I'm grateful for.*

♥ When I *sit down to have my cup of coffee*, I will *write down my daily to-do list.*

Workdays self-care

♥ When I *get to my workplace*, I will *take the stairs rather than the lift.*

♥ When I *sit at my desk*, I will *drink a glass of water.*

Evening self-care

♥ When I *get home from work*, I will *send a message to my best friend.*

♥ When I *sit on my bed*, I will *meditate for five minutes.*

Hard days self-care

When I *start to feel too pressured*, I will *schedule in my recovery time*.

When I *feel down*, I will *reach out to a trusted person*.

Weekend self-care

When I *find some spare time*, I will *plan a road trip*.

When I *finish my weekend to-dos*, I will *visit my loved ones*.

If you take anything away from this book, let it be this – It's the small things that make a difference, the seemingly unimportant choices you make daily and those little habits that build up to create your overall health and happiness. Be proud of all the hard work and intention you put into taking care of yourself, no matter how bumpy your self-care journey is. This is what self-love looks like.

1 3 5 7 9 10 8 6 4 2

Pop Press, an imprint of Ebury Publishing,
20 Vauxhall Bridge Road, London SW1V 2SA

Pop Press is part of the Penguin Random House group of companies
whose addresses can be found at global.penguinrandomhouse.com

Penguin
Random House
UK

First published by Pop Press in 2022

www.penguin.co.uk

A CIP catalogue record for this book is available from the British Library

ISBN 9781529149630

Interior designed by Georgie Hewitt
Illustrations by Color me Happii by Kaitlyn
Printed and Bound in Latvia by Livonia Print SIA

Penguin Random House is committed to a sustainable future for our
business, our readers and our planet. This book is made from Forest
Stewardship Council® certified paper.

The authorised representative in the EEA is Penguin Random House
Ireland, Morrison Chambers, 32 Nassau Street, Dublin D02 YH68.